How to play

SOC

a step·by·step guide

Text:
Liz French

Technical consultant:
Kit Carson
Youth Development Officer
Peterborough United FC

JARROLD

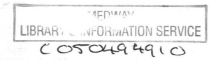

Other titles in this series are:

AMERICAN FOOTBALL   **HOCKEY**
BADMINTON   **SAILING A DINGHY**
BASKETBALL   **SNOOKER**
BOWLS   **SQUASH**
COARSE FISHING   **SWIMMING**
CRICKET   **TABLE TENNIS**
CROQUET   **TENNIS**
GET FIT FOR SPORT   **TABLE TENNIS**
GOLF   **WINDSURFING**

How to play SOCCER
ISBN 0-7117-0513-5

Text © Liz French 1991
This edition © Jarrold Publishing 1991
Illustrations by Malcolm Ryan

First published 1991
Reprinted 1996

Designed and produced by
Parke Sutton Limited, Norwich
for Jarrold Publishing, Norwich
Printed in Great Britain. 3/96

Contents

Introduction

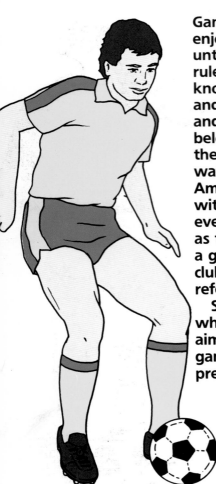

Games involving kicking a ball have been enjoyed for thousands of years, but it was not until the middle of the last century that the rules were laid down for the game as we now know it. Today, soccer is a truly international and universal game, the most widely played and watched sport of all. Almost 150 nations belong to *FIFA*, the world governing body for the game — and the last World Cup Final was watched by 1.7 billion people on TV! Amazingly, its popularity continues to grow, with more young players and more clubs than ever before. It is also a game for girls as much as for boys, and women's football is enjoying a growing popularity in schools, colleges and clubs. (Note that for simplicity, players are referred to as 'he' throughout this book).

Soccer's appeal lies partly in its simplicity — what could be easier to understand than the aim of scoring a goal — and yet it is also a game of great subtlety and skill. It is a game of precision and stamina rather than brute force.

And it is also, of course, great fun to play and exciting to watch. To be a good player, determination, enthusiasm and the ability to work as part of a team are just as important as natural talent. Whether you aspire to be a great player with an international side, or simply want to get more out of a game with your friends, good practice and a sound understanding of the elements of the game will help you reach your potential. This book covers the basics of soccer, and will help you develop your game and become a better team member. There are sections on technique and tactics, and plenty of tips for effective practice. The glossary on page 48 will help with any unfamiliar words encountered in the text; these appear in italics as they appear in the book.

Of course, no book can take the place of a good coach, and if you want to develop your game further, remember that clubs always welcome good, keen players. You'll find your county or city Regional Football Association in the phone book, and they will produce a handbook listing all their affiliated clubs. You can also get information on national, regional and local coaching schemes from The Football Association, 16 Lancaster Gate, London W2 3LW.

PITCH AND EQUIPMENT

The Pitch

Football can be played on almost any fairly level area, but ideally the pitch should be of level grass, or artificial grass. The main diagram here shows the markings on the pitch. The size of the pitch itself can vary, but it must always be longer than it is wide.

maximum 130 yds (118.8 m)
minimum 100 yds (91.4 m)

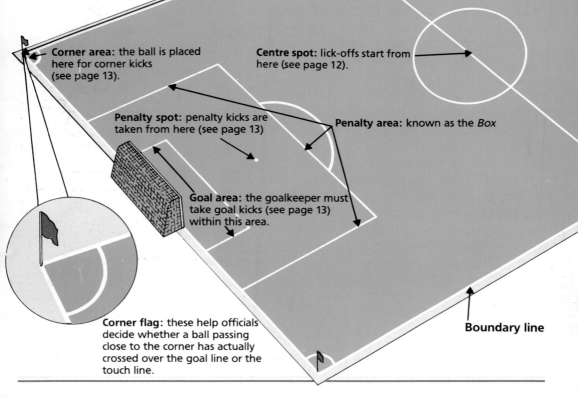

Halfway line: divides the pitch into two equal areas of play; may be marked at each end by flagposts placed a yard outside the field of play.

Corner area: the ball is placed here for corner kicks (see page 13).

Centre spot: lick-offs start from here (see page 12).

Penalty spot: penalty kicks are taken from here (see page 13)

Penalty area: known as the *Box*

Goal area: the goalkeeper must take goal kicks (see page 13) within this area.

Corner flag: these help officials decide whether a ball passing close to the corner has actually crossed over the goal line or the touch line.

Boundary line

Goal

maximum 100 yds (91.4 m)
minimum 50 yds (45.7 m)

Penalty arc: known as the *D*.
When a penalty kick is being
taken other players must be
outside this arc as well as outside
the penalty area itself.

Goal line

All boundary lines and other
markings are 5in (0.12m) wide
and form part of the field of
play.

The ball

Official matches are played with a standard
leather ball which must be of a certain size
and weight. It is worth buying one of your
own to practise with, but you may prefer one
of the slightly smaller balls available in sports
shops. Choose one with a waterproof surface
which will not pick up mud and water. A
white waterproofed ball is useful on dull
winter days, being easier to see than a
darker colour.

The goals

The goals are 8ft (2.4m) high. They consist of
two upright goalposts placed 8yds (7.32m)
apart and joined at the top by a crossbar.
Posts and crossbar are made of wood or metal
and painted white, and nets are usually fitted
to the back to show clearly when a goal has
been scored.

8 ft

8 yds

Dress

Boots

Your boots are the most important part of your kit and must fit properly if they are to be comfortable for a whole match. Any good sports shop will sell a wide range of well-constructed boots, and will give advice on correct fitting, but here are a few tips:

- Do choose leather for good all-round protection.

- Try on boots of different makes — they vary in width and construction.

- When trying on boots, always lace them up properly and stand up in them.

- If your feet are still growing, allow a *little* room for growth, but don't buy a size too big.

Good quality trainers are fine for practice:

- Again, do buy from a reputable sports shop.

- Leather uppers give better protection when kicking.

- Soles with a deep tread will give you better grip.

Your choice of boot is really a question of personal preference and it's good fun checking out what your favourite players are wearing too!

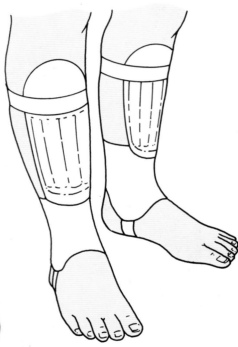

Shin guards

These are compulsory for official matches and are sensible for all games to protect your shins from the inevitable bangs and scrapes. Choose a comfortable, lightweight pair.

Clothing

For match play, of course, players of the same team all wear the same colour shirt, except for the goalkeeper. They must also wear identical shorts and socks and be numbered according to their position on the field. For practice with friends, it doesn't much matter what colours you wear, although for team play it makes sense to wear a similar kit for easy identification.

Goalkeeper's protective clothing

Goalkeepers need extra protection, and padded clothing to protect hips, elbows and shoulders is advisable. Goalies often wear special gloves for protection and to give a better grip on the ball: there will be a range to choose from in any good sports shop. A sweatshirt or tracksuit top is also vital in cold weather because the goalie runs around less than the other players.

Typical numbering system:

1. Goalkeeper
2. Full back (right back) or right full back
3. Full back (left back) or left full back
4. Right midfield
5. Right centre-back
6. Left centre-back
7. Outside right (winger)
8. Left midfield
9. Centre-forward right (striker)
10. Centre-forward left (striker)
11. Outside left (winger)
12/13. Substitutes

THE GAME

The aim of the game

Soccer is basically a very simple game played between two teams. The teams each try to get and keep possession of the ball and kick or head it into their opponents' goal. The winning team is the one which has scored the most goals.

The Players

Practice games are often played with only five or six players on each team, but the full team consists of eleven players, one of whom is the goalkeeper.

The teams are made up of one goalkeeper (see pages 34-7) and a number of defenders, midfielders and attackers. In the past, and until the 1950s, each team member had a specific role, but today the actual positions of the players are not fixed and every player must be able to attack and defend. Team formations will vary. The diagram opposite shows a typical 4-2-4 formation. This means that there are four strikers or forwards, two midfielders and four backs. Other typical formations include the 4-3-3 and 4-4-2.

No hands

Except for the goalkeeper, players must not use hands or arms to control or propel the ball in soccer.

Defenders

These are the back players whose job is to stop opposing players from getting into scoring positions, and to support their own goalkeeper. They must also be ready to start attacks as soon as they gain possession.

Midfielders

Playing in the middle of the field, these players form the link between defence and attack.

Attackers

Their most important job is to score goals but they must be defensive minded as well.

Substitutes

Teams may also have two named substitutes who may take the place of any player during a match, at the discretion of the team manager. Once a player has been replaced by a substitute, he may not re-enter the game.

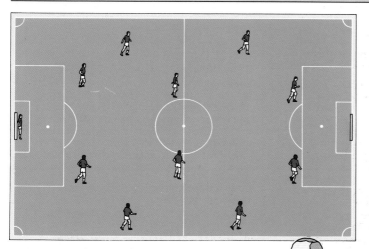

A typical 4-2-4 formation: four strikers, two midfielders and four defenders.

The Officials

In match play, there are three officials responsible for the control of the game.

The Referee: whose job is to enforce the laws of the game and act as timekeeper. He uses a whistle to stop play when necessary.

Two Linesmen: who patrol the touchlines and let the referee know (by waving a flag) when the ball has passed over the touchline or goal line, and which team is entitled to the throw-in (see page 13).

The rules

Get a copy of the Laws of the Game (available from most clubs, or contact the F.A., address on page 5). Familiarity with the rules will help your game.

RULE BOOK

Playing the Game

Duration

A full match lasts ninety minutes, with play divided into two 45-minute periods separated by a five- or ten-minute interval. The teams change ends after the interval. The referee may add on extra time at half-time or the end of the match to compensate for time lost through injuries or time-wasting.

The kick-off

● At the kick-off the ball is placed on the centre spot, and the team kicking off must all be on their side of the halfway line as the kick is made. The opposing players must all be at least ten yards (9.15m) from the ball — that means outside the centre circle.

● The ball is in play when it has travelled a distance equal to its own circumference (about 68.5cm, 27ins).

● The player who kicked off must not kick the ball again until another player has touched it.

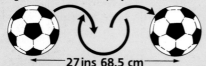

27ins 68.5 cm

The kick-off procedure is repeated:

● At the beginning of the second half (the team who did NOT kick off at the start does so now).

● After a goal (the team who conceded the goal take the kick-off).

Starting

A coin is tossed, with the winner of the toss deciding either to kick off or to choose ends for the first half. This choice can be quite important, because it allows a team to take advantage of weather conditions at the start of the match. However, teams change ends after half-time, and the team which did not kick off at the start now has the right to do so.

Ball in play

The ball continues to be in play until:

● A goal is scored, **or**

● The ball passes over the touch line or goal line, **or**

● The referee stops play.

Always play on until you hear the whistle.

Scoring a goal

For a goal to be allowed, all of the ball must have crossed all of the goal line between the goal posts. It makes no difference whether the ball is played intentionally or by accident, by an attacking or a defending team member — provided it is not handled by an attacker.

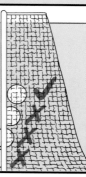

What if . . . a defending player sends the ball into the goal with his hand or arm?
This counts as an 'own goal' — a goal against the defending side.

When the ball leaves the field

When the ball crosses over the boundary lines it is out of play and the referee will blow his whistle. What happens next depends on which part of the boundary it crossed and who last touched the ball.

   If an attacking player sends the ball over the touchline, a throw-in is taken by any defending player and vice versa.

   If the ball crosses the goal-line — except when it goes in the goal itself — the result is either a goal kick (if the attacking team last touched it) or a corner kick (if a defender had last touch).

Throw-in

● Taken from as close as possible to the spot where the ball crossed the line.

● Player must face the pitch and must have both feet on the ground and behind the line.

● Player holds the ball in both hands and throws it back into play from behind and over his head.

Corner kick

● Taken from the quarter circle (quadrant) marking on the corner nearest to the point where the ball went out.

● Defenders may not come within 10yds (9.15m) of the quadrant until the kick has been taken.

● The player taking the kick may not play the ball again until it has been touched by another player.

Goal kick

● Normally taken by the goalkeeper.

● Taken from the line of the 6 yd box nearest to where the ball went out.

● Ball is not in play until it has passed out of the penalty area.

● The goal kick is taken again if any player plays the ball before it leaves the penalty area.

● A goal may not be scored direct from a goal kick.

Offences and Free Kicks

When an infringement of the laws occurs, the referee stops play and restarts with a free kick to the non-offending team. Free kicks can be either direct or indirect, and are taken from the spot where the offence occurred. If a serious infringement occurs in the penalty area, a direct free kick at the goal (a Penalty) is awarded.

Direct free kick

These are awarded for the more serious offences shown opposite. A goal may be scored from a direct free kick without another player touching the ball.

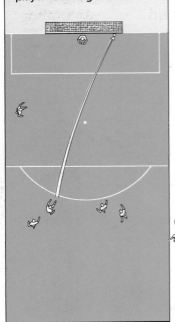

Indirect free kick

These are awarded for less serious offences, including breaches of the offside rule (see pages 16-17). Other examples include obstructing an opponent, and the goalkeeper in his penalty area handling the ball kicked to him by a team-mate.

Another player must play the ball before a goal can be scored. The referee indicates an indirect free kick by raising his hand and keeping it raised until a second player has touched the ball.

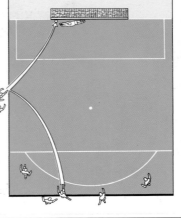

Penalty kick

When a penalty kick is taken, only the goalkeeper and the player taking the kick are allowed in the penalty area.

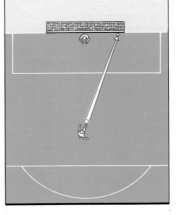

What if . . . a penalty is awarded just as the whistle goes for half time or the end of the match?
Extra time is allowed for the penalty to be taken.

There are nine offences serious enough to incur a direct free kick (or penalty if in the penalty area): eight are *fouls* against your opponents as shown here; the ninth is handling the ball deliberately, which is defined as 'carrying, propelling or striking the ball with the hand or arm'.

1 Charging an opponent in a violent or dangerous way

You can charge fairly with your *shoulders* if the ball is within playing distance of you and your opponent and you are both definitely trying to play the ball. But using your elbow is *not* allowed.

2 Charging an opponent from behind

(Unless he is obstructing you).

3 Holding an opponent

You must not use your hands or arms to hold back an opponent.

4 Pushing an opponent

You must not push an opponent with your hands or arms.

5 Tripping or throwing an opponent

The referee can usually distinguish whether someone is tripped up intentionally or accidentally.

6 Jumping at an opponent

You mustn't jump with both feet at the ball when it is being played by an opponent.

7 Kicking or attempting to kick an opponent

8 Striking or attempting to strike an opponent, or spitting at him

1   2   3   4

Offside

The offside rule is designed to stop players from waiting in front of their opponents' goal for a pass, ready to shoot at close range. The rule itself is quite simple, but it often

The rule says

● **You are in an offside position** if you are in your opponents' half of the field when the ball is played, and nearer to the goal line than the ball is UNLESS
you are no nearer your opponents' goal line than at least two of your opponents — this can include the goalkeeper.
Note: this is a new ruling (1990). Previously you had to have two players **between** you and the goal — now you are allowed to be level with the defender/s.

● **If you are in an offside position,** you become truly offside at the moment the ball is played by your team-mate — not at the moment you receive it.

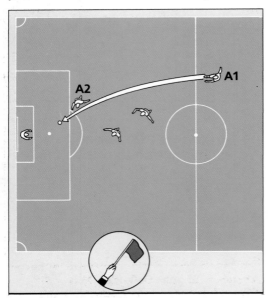

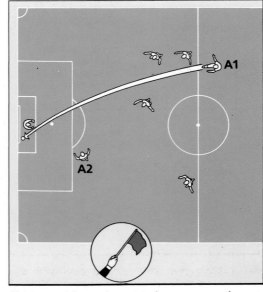

In both diagrams attacker A2 is standing in an offside position when A1 shoots to goal — because there is only a goalie between A2 and the goal.

causes discussion and sometimes argument — mainly because the referee so often has to use his discretion in deciding whether or not an offence has occurred. Offside offences result in a stoppage of play, and an indirect free kick to the non-offending side.

Not offside

Even if you are in an offside position, you will not be penalised:

● If you are not involved in the play at the time, and are not attempting to play the ball, obstructing an opponent or otherwise interfering with the play.

● If the ball was last touched or played by an opponent.

● If you receive the ball direct from a corner kick, a goal kick or a throw-in.

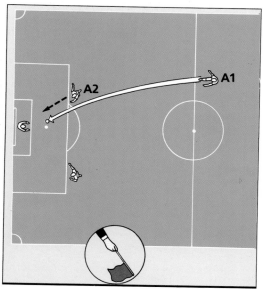

Not offside. Here player A2 is level with the second last defender at the moment the ball is played. Under new ruling (1990) this is not offside.

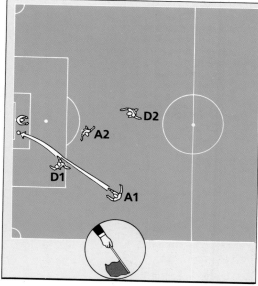

A1 shoots to goal. Defender D1 is situated between the attackers A1 and A2 and the goalie — putting him onside.

Passing

Passing the ball is one of the most important of all soccer skills. For a team to achieve success, its members must be able to pass accurately to each other. A pass obviously involves two players — one making the pass and the other receiving it. Constant practice is the only way to develop good passing techniques.

There are three basic elements to concentrate on:

Weighting

This simply means the amount of power you put in: it needs to be just enough. Too much and you'll either miss your target or the ball will be travelling too fast for your team-mate to control when it reaches him. Too little weighting and the ball will not reach its target.

Direction

You need a great deal of practice to develop accuracy in the direction of your passes.

1. Before the pass you need to keep your head up to be aware of exactly where you are aiming.

2. As you play the ball, keep your head still, and your eyes concentrated on the ball. The toe and knee of your support leg (the one NOT kicking) must point straight at your target.

Timing

Remember that the player you are passing to will be moving — so you need to aim at the spot where he will be when he receives your pass. If you are the receiving player, concentrate on anticipating where the ball is going to be and getting yourself into position for receiving it and passing it on.

Low or high pass?

Passes are easier to control and receive if they travel along the ground. To keep the ball low:

● Strike the ball through its top half.

● Have your support foot alongside the ball but just a few inches away.

Sometimes you will need to get the ball into the air to get past the opposition — this is an overhead pass. To loft the ball high:

● Stab at the ball, striking it through its bottom half.

● Have your support foot at the side of the ball but further back.

Hint box: Passing

● During a game, constantly ask yourself, 'what would I do with the ball if I had it now?'

● Always be aware of where your team members are.

● When you have made the pass — MOVE to a position where you can take a return pass.

● Don't let your opponent come too close before passing — no more than a yard or two.

● Think 'triangles' (see page 38).

Hint box: Which foot?

Just as you are either left- or right-handed, you will find kicking easier and more natural with one foot than with the other. During a game, you will tend to use your natural foot more often. Practise and train on your weak foot so that during a game you won't waste precious seconds adjusting your position because you lack confidence on your weaker side.

You can pass with your chest and head as well as your foot (see ball control, pages 24-25). But most passes are made with your feet, so practise all the techniques shown here.

Using the inside of your foot

The most accurate short passes are made by using the inside of your foot. This is often called a 'push pass' and can cover most directions (except behind you — see back heel, page 22) but only limited distances. Practise aiming at targets in front and to your sides and from different distances up to about 25 yds (23 m).

1 Along the ground

- Support foot alongside the ball, pointing in the direction of the pass.

- Kicking foot at right angles to the body and the line of the ball.

- Toes turned out, ankles firm.

- Strike the ball in its centre.

- Head still and over the ball — eyes on the ball.

- Follow through with your kicking foot.

2 Into the air

Position as before but:

- Lean back a little.

- Support foot slightly behind the ball.

- Contact made at the centre of the bottom of the ball.

3 Volley

To pass while the ball is still in the air:

- Turn your toes out and stab at the ball.

- Get your body over the ball to keep it low.

Using the top of your foot

If you need to give the ball more distance, you can lob the ball using the top of your foot: known as 'hitting off the laces'.

- Support foot is level with the ball but further away.

- Swing your kicking foot back well before striking.

- Contact made with the centre of the bottom of the ball.

- Good follow-through.

Using the outside of your foot

This is useful especially when making diagonal passes to your team-mates when there is an opponent right in front of you.

- Support foot is a little behind your kicking foot and further to the side.

- With toes pointing inwards, punch the ball centrally.

- Keep follow-through short and low.

The chipped pass

This pass lifts the ball high, but backspin and lack of follow-through make it drop straight down. Useful for passing to a team member over the heads of your opponents.

● Support foot is next to the ball.

● Lean back.

● Chip the ball off the laces through its bottom half.

● Little or no follow-through.

The drive pass

Similar to a lob pass, this is a pass for distance and power, especially when the ball is stationary (a *dead ball*).

● Kicking foot pointing downwards.

● Knee over the ball.

● Strike the ball off the laces.

The back heel

Normally it makes sense to pass the way you are facing, but if you are sure there is a team mate behind you ready to take your pass, you can try this and surprise your opponents.

● Support foot alongside ball.

● Kicking foot comes over the ball and flicks it backwards.

The wall pass

Here one player uses another as a 'wall' to bounce the ball back as he runs past a defender.

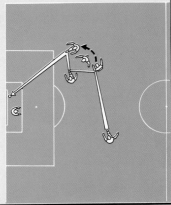

Bending the ball in flight

This fairly advanced technique involves putting sidespin on the ball, and will take a lot of practice. It is very useful for swinging the ball past your opponents, and especially for getting around the end of a defensive wall in front of a goal (see page 41).

- Support foot is behind the ball.

- Toe of kicking foot points straight ahead and contact is made with the side of the foot.

- Kick low on the side of the ball.

- Good follow-through is needed.

You can bend the ball using the inside of your foot . . .

. . . or the outside of your foot.

Hint box: which pass to use?

When you get possession of the ball, you have to think very quickly to decide the best pass to go for, weighing up the various options and factors:

- Do you need to keep running? If so, it can be easier to use the outside of your foot. This also helps to disguise your pass.

- If you have time to check your stride, you'll get better accuracy from the inside of your foot.

- Do you need to cover a long distance? You'll need a lob pass or a drive pass off the laces.

- If a short pass is needed, use the inside of your foot for better control and accuracy.

Where are you in the field? It helps to think of the pitch divided into thirds. As a very general rule, you'll need long passes in the defending third, to get the ball away from your own goal area. Short passes can be played anywhere, but are more common in the middle third or attacking third.

Controlling The Ball

Developing good control and a 'feel' for the ball is essential to your game and only comes through constant practice with the ball. See page 47 for some ideas for practising on your

Hint box: ball control basics

These rules apply whatever part of your body you are using.

Prepare:

● LINE UP with the ball early.

● DECIDE which part of your body will stop the ball.

● WATCH the ball all the time.

On impact:

● RELAX that part of the body in the direction the ball is travelling to 'cushion' its flight and take the pace off it.

● LOOK up to check on your next move.

● CONTROL the ball to your side ready to act.

Ball control with your feet
Practise all these with both feet

1 Inside of foot

● Your weight is on your support leg.

● Toes point out to make impact area as large as possible.

● On impact, foot moves back.

● Use your arms to balance.

2 Outside of foot

● As before, but toes point inwards.

3 Top of the foot

Especially useful for controlling a dropping ball.

● As before, but 'catch' the ball on your laces.

own. A good player can quickly control a ball coming from any direction, angle or height, and uses almost all parts of the body, except hands and arms of course!

Controlling the ball with your thigh . . .

- Support foot is firmly on the ground, leg flexed a little.

- Lift your thigh as high as you need to, depending on the height of the ball.

- Cushion the ball by withdrawing your thigh and allowing it to drop to the ground.

- You can sometimes pass straight from your thigh, push—ing the ball away with a punching movement.

. . . your midriff

- Useful for stopping a ball that has bounced in front of you.

- Legs well apart.

- Tense your stomach muscles and lean forward from the hips for impact.

- Use your arms to balance.

. . . your chest

- Useful for trapping a descending high ball.

- Legs firmly placed.

- Lean back on impact to absorb the pace of the ball.

. . . and your head

- Needs lots of practice and good timing.

- Get right under the descending ball.

- Keep your eyes open all the time.

- At impact, bend your knees to take the speed out of the ball.

- See page 30 for more on heading.

Shooting

Football is basically all about goal scoring, and understanding good shooting practice is as important as an instinctive ability. So here is the basic how, when and where of shooting.

How?

There are three basic steps to shooting:

1 When you get the ball, look up quickly and assess the positions of the defence, the goalkeeper and the goal itself.

2 Decide on the exact direction and force of your shot.

3 Keep your eyes on the ball and SHOOT!

Keep the ball low

Low shots are nearly always best for shooting.

- Get in line with the ball.

- Your support foot is next to the ball, knee pointing at your target.

- Kicking foot points down.

- Keep your head still and down, over the ball.

- Contact is made with the middle of the ball.

- Keep your eyes on the ball.

- Follow through in the direction you're aiming at.

What if . . . you keep missing your target?

Don't give up — keep practising and check through all the basics again.

If the ball is low but going wide:

- Is your support foot pointing the right way?

- Are you hitting through the centre of the ball?

- Are your eyes on the ball all the time?

If the ball is going high:

- Make sure you're not stretching to shoot — get in line with the ball quickly.

- Is your head down, with eyes on the ball at impact?

- Make sure you're not hitting the ball underneath.

When?

DO shoot

● Whenever you have a chance or even a half chance.

● Quickly — you need a balance between using your instincts and weighing up the possibilities. Delay too long and you'll miss your chance!

DON'T shoot:

● If the choice is between a really difficult goal attempt or passing to a team-mate who's in a better position.

● If you are further than about 35 yds (30m) from the goal.

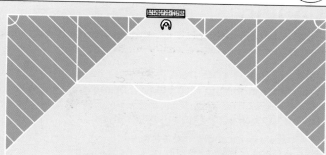

Imaginary lines have been drawn from the goal posts to the corners of the penalty box. If you are in the shaded area, it's best to pass the ball to a colleague or move to a better position. Otherwise, go for it!

Where?

● Aim for the far half of the goal — shots going away from the goalkeeper are harder to save; and even if a save *is* made, there is likely to be a second chance at scoring.

● Shots from directly in front of the goal are harder for the goalkeeper to read because you can aim at any point of the goal.

● Shoot diagonally across the goalkeeper if possible.

● If no part of the goal is undefended, send your shot low and close to the goal keeper's legs — he'll have less control.

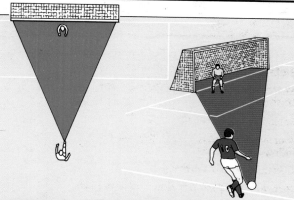

The player in front of the goal has a wide choice of angles (shaded red). Player 10, at the side, is more limited and easier for the goalkeeper to read, (shaded brown).

Running

Football is an athletic sport and running with and without the ball are essential elements of the game.

Running with the ball
This can mean dribbling (see below), or moving the ball across undefended areas.

Moving the ball across undefended areas

● If you see a space, move into it fast.

● You must kick the ball far enough to let you keep up your speed — but not so far that you can't control it if you are challenged.

● Look up when you are running and down at the ball when you touch it — and keep touches to a minimum.

Dribbling

Dribbling involves keeping the ball under control as you get past defenders to create space to pass to a colleague or to shoot.

It is risky to dribble in or near your own penalty area or when you are outnumbered by defenders.

● Always try to stay between the ball and your challenger.

● Use the inside and outside of your foot to keep the ball close.

● Use a 'split glance' — looking up to check where you are going and the position of others, then down at the ball.

Hint box: dribbling

● Practise turning with the ball — watch how the experts do it and copy.

● Put your foot on the ball if you can't run on — this is *screening* — but you must keep the ball moving to avoid a foul.

● Try to make your dribbling deceptive by pretending to go one way and actually turning another (*feinting*).

● Dribbling is risky — so if you can make a safe pass instead, do so.

Running without the ball

This is important too, especially when you realise that during an average game, you will only have possession of the ball for about three minutes! The rest of the time, you should:

● Watch the ball.

● Keep moving.

● Look for space and move into it to give the player on the ball passing options.

● In defence, watch for chances to gain possession.

● When you get the ball, use it well and then start again.

Heading

An ability to head the ball accurately and confidently will give you the edge over many players. Heading can be broadly divided into two main kinds: attacking heading, to create goal opportunities or shoot at the goal; and defensive heading, to gain possession and start attacks.

For both categories the basic technique is the same:

1

As the ball approaches, line up to it quickly.

2

Look quickly to see where you are going to head it to, but otherwise keep your eye on the ball. It is natural for your eyes to close momentarily at impact.

3

Take the ball on the middle of your forehead. Keep your neck, back and upper body firm.

Hint box: good heading

● Don't be afraid of the ball: it won't hurt you if you use your forehead.

● Don't jump for a ball if you can head it from the ground.

● When you do need height, get a bit extra by thrusting one or both arms down quickly.

● To increase the power of a header, lean backwards before impact and then throw yourself forward and upwards towards the ball.

● Don't head for the sake of it — it should always have a purpose.

● Attack the ball: don't let it attack you.

● Practise heading at first by throwing the ball to yourself.

Attacking heading

Here your aim is to head the ball to a team-mate or shoot for a goal. Either way, don't wait for the ball to come to you — run into a suitable position and get in line with it while it is still in the air.

Shooting

● Dropping headers are the hardest for goalkeepers, so aim to contact the ball in the middle of its top half so as to send it downwards.

● Time your run and jump so that you head the ball at the highest point of your jump.

Passing

● If you can't get to the goal, use your header to deflect the ball sideways to a team-mate.

● Go for the shot as before, but at the moment of impact, twist your head to send the ball sideways.

● To get to a team-mate behind you, contact the ball in the middle of its bottom half and flick your head back.

Defensive heading

With defensive heading, your aim is to get the ball well away from your own goal, so your headers need to be high and powerful.

● Line up as before and time your jump so that you contact the ball at the highest possible point.

● Take off on one leg only.

● Keep your eyes fixed firmly on the ball.

● Thrust your arms down as you jump to give yourself maximum height.

● Your head and body should lean backwards.

● Throw yourself forwards at the ball so that you achieve a punching action with as much weight as possible.

● Contact the ball on its midline or bottom line for maximum height.

● Follow through.

Defence Skills

When your team loses possession of the ball, you must all work together to get it back. The easiest way is to intercept a pass made by one opponent to another, but marking, jockeying and tackling are all important defence skills too.

Marking

Marking is a vital part of your team's effort to regain the ball. It means staying close to an opponent to make it hard for him to receive a pass or to get away from you.

- Mark one opponent.

- Always try to be between him and the ball.

- Don't lose concentration — be aware of other players' positions.

- Always ask yourself 'What would I do with the ball if I got it now?'

Jockeying

If your opponent does get the ball, act fast. If you can't intercept it, make it hard for him to play it by tackling (see opposite) or jockeying him into making a mistake. Jockeying means putting yourself at the right angle to force your opponent where you want him to go. You need to be in a semi-crouched position for this, with your head still and watching the ball all the time.

Tackling

Tackling means using your feet to win the ball from an opponent, and is an important part of the game. There are three main types of tackle:

1. The block

A block tackle is made from an upright position, from in front or from the side. Aim to touch the ball with the inside of your foot just as your opponent plays it. Keep your knees bent to take the impact.

2. The sliding tackle

This is a fairly desperate measure since it leaves you lying on the ground! It is usually used by the back defence players when chasing an attacker who has run clear. Aim to get as close to your target as possible and keep your tackling leg close to the ground and slightly flexed. Remember you can't slide tackle from behind the player.

3. The toe-away tackle

If you are defending against a forward who has his back to you, always watch for chances to stick your foot out and send the ball away from him with your toe.

Hint box: successful tackling

Mental attitude is important here. Once you go in to tackle, be positive and confident.

● **Get your full bodyweight behind the tackle and follow through well.**

● **Be careful to tackle the *ball*, never your opponent's foot, or you'll give away a foul.**

Goalkeeping

Goalkeeping is a specialist job requiring strength, bravery, quick reactions and agility. It needs a good understanding of *angles* (see page 36). It also demands a safe pair of hands and a strong voice! The goalkeeper is actually the last line of defence and the first line of attack, and defending the goal is only part of his job.

Functions of the goalkeeper

The goalkeeper's job can be broadly categorised into three areas:

1. Defending the goal

This is the obvious one, but it means more than leaping to save a goal.

● Keep your eyes on the game all the time and don't let your concentration slip.

● Be aware of where your opponents and your team-mates are at any time, and what styles of play they are using.

● Watch the wind direction and pitch surface because these will affect the play.

2. Starting attack

When you have possession of the ball remember that your job is not just to throw or kick it out of danger — you have a positive chance to start an attack.

● Practise your kicking and throwing constantly.

● Never throw to a marked team-mate.

● Take care to weight the ball accurately.

3. Organising the defence

Remember that you are in a unique position, facing the game and able to see exactly what is going on.

● Be in control of the box.

● Use your voice! Call, warn and advise your defence players continually.

● Be confident, so team-mates respect your calls.

Catching

Catching the ball confidently and safely is one of the basics of good goalkeeping. And once you've got the ball, you mustn't drop it!

● Try to get your body and hands behind the ball as it arrives.

● Use both hands whenever possible.

● Keep your eye on the ball.

● Make a 'basket' for the ball with both hands, fingers spread.

● Keep your hands firm but not rigid.

● As soon as you touch the ball, bend your elbows and pull it into your body.

● Crosses and corners are the hardest shots to catch — good positioning is vital and you should run to meet the ball, not wait for it to come to you.

1. Crouch to receive low shots.

2. Stand with legs together for medium height shots.

3. Jump for high shots if necessary, and try to use both hands.

Angles

Goalkeepers need to know how to 'narrow the angle' so the opponent has the smallest possible target. Timing is vital and will only come with practice.

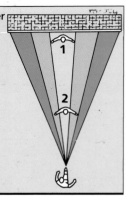

1 With the goalkeeper on the line (1) the striker has a wide choice of angles. Move forward (2) and the angles are much more limited.

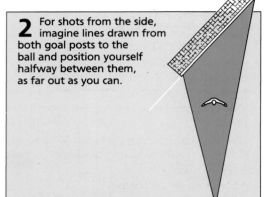

2 For shots from the side, imagine lines drawn from both goal posts to the ball and position yourself halfway between them, as far out as you can.

Throwing the ball

Distributing the ball effectively once you have gained possession is vital. You can either kick or throw it — but throwing is easier to control. Your main aim always is to give the receiver an easily controlled ball.

● Too hard a throw is difficult to control.

● Too slow a throw will be intercepted by an opponent.

● Hit the ground well in front of the receiver so the ball travels along the ground and is easier for him to control.

● For long throws, use an overarm action.

● For shorter throws, use an underarm action.

Punching

Always catch a ball if you can, but if it is just out of reach, punch instead:

- Use two fists where possible.

- Keep your eyes on the ball.

- Try to touch the ball at the highest point.

- Use a short, sharp punch *through* the ball on its mid-line, or, for more height, on its lower half.

Diving

There will be occasions when you have to dive to the side to save a goal.

- Timing is vital.

- Keep your eye on the ball.

- Have your weight on the leg nearer to the ball direction.

- Throw your body to get in line with the ball.

- Get your bottom hand behind the ball first, with the other hand following and landing on top of it.

- Get your body behind the ball as well if you can.

Turning the ball over the crossbar

If you are under challenge, or can't reach to catch or punch a ball, you can try to turn it over the bar:

- Use your palm and fingers.

- If possible, contact the ball while it is higher than the crossbar.

- Knock it over, don't flick it.

General Tactics

Football is a tactical game and outwitting your opponents can be vital to your team's success. Tactics is all about teamwork: individual skill is important, of course, but never forget that you are part of a team.

Planning a match

Good teams use well-rehearsed set pieces, especially when taking free kicks, corners, throw-ins and penalties. The team coach or manager decides on the tactics for a game — but the plan often changes or is modified at half-time, depending on how the match is going!

Even if you are playing a five- or six-a-side game with friends, it's worth working out some ideas of how to play certain situations. But be prepared to think quickly and adapt your plans if your opponents 'read' what you are doing.

Think triangles

Watch the path the ball takes as it is played from player to player during a match and you'll see that it's easier to keep possession by passing in a zigzag pattern than in a straight line. So 'think triangles'.

Imagine you are Player A. Your team-mate B has passed the ball to C but C can't pass to you because you're marked.

By moving as shown, you have made yourself an effective point of a triangle, ready to receive the pass.

Goal Tactics

Some general hints on where and when to shoot were outlined on page 27. Here are some tactical ploys for goal attempts. You'll need to practise these often with your team-mates to make them work.

1 Crosses into the box

This is a useful way of setting up shooting opportunities, especially if your team has a powerful striker to win the ball. A winger, wide midfielder or even *overlapping* full back sends the ball across into the box for an oncoming player who then either goes for goal or controls the ball and sends it to a team-mate to shoot, as shown here. The run into the box has to be timed to perfection to meet the ball. Practise these moves with your team-mates often.

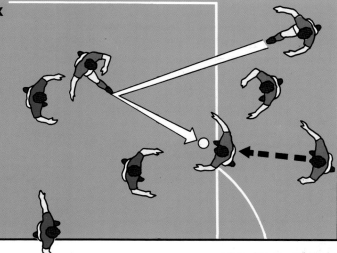

2 Wall pass

If you're quick and alert you may be able to catch defenders off guard with a well-worked, well-practised *wall pass*. The idea is to give the attacker possession a split second before he is marked again, to enable him to shoot.

3 Long shots

Long shots practised in training can catch the goalkeeper unawares but you need confidence to let the ball fly from beyond the box. You can also *feint* going round the defenders and then suddenly cut inside and shoot for goal.

4 Goal poaching

Having a player stationed near the goal line often leads to scoring chances. He's there to pounce if the keeper should drop or fail to hold the ball for a split second. He also picks up the pieces from long shots, goalmouth scrambles and defenders' mistakes — and in fact makes himself a general all-round nuisance to the defenders.

Throw-in Tactics

Think of a throw-in as a kind of pass. A good passer makes it easy for the receiver to control the ball — and the same goes for throws:

● **Make sure the ball goes to his feet at a pace that's easy to control.**

● **Don't let it hit the ground at speed and bounce up around the waist of the receiver.**

● **A recent development in football is the long throw. If you or someone in your team can perfect this skill, a long throw can be as dangerous as a corner.**

How you play a throw-in depends on what part of the field you are in.

In the defensive third:
Here retaining possession is your main priority.

● Don't throw the ball square into the field where lost possession gives your opponents a clear run at the goal.

● Throw at an angle of no more than 30° to the line.

In the middle third:
The danger of losing possession is not so acute.

● Don't be slow at taking the throw — a quick throw before the opposition can mark up can create an attacking situation.

● Don't stand too close to the thrower because if you do you can easily be closed down.

● Move into space — you can create space for others and begin an attack.

In the attacking third:
Here you should use the throw to penetrate the opposition defence. Practise different routines with your friends — this picture shows a simple one you could try.

A1 and A2 are standing together on the edge of the box with their markers. A2 darts forward as if to receive the ball. But the ball is thrown to A1 who then immediately passes the ball into the path of A2 who has turned ready to collect the pass.

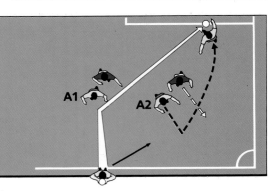

Free Kick Tactics

Most soccer fans associate free kicks with brilliant individual efforts close to goal. In fact the famous Brazilians made free kicks one of the most exciting aspects of the modern game with brilliant goals which seemed to come from nowhere. Watch any good team and you'll see that their free kicks are well thought out with everyone knowing what to do.

● Because opposing players have to be 10 yds (9.15 m) from the ball the kicker has time and little pressure on him. But remember that if you take too long to prepare, the opposition will mark up. This is why a quick free kick is often taken.

● Be aware of wind conditions when preparing to kick — it will affect the amount of weighting you put on it.

What you do with a free kick depends on where you are:

In the defensive or middle thirds — retaining possession is your priority.

In the attacking third — try to set up a scoring opportunity.

Free kicks close to goal:

● Don't make it too complicated. The more people involved, the more likely it is that errors will be made.

● Check that everyone involved knows their role.

● Make sure the kick is taken by the player who's best at shooting or passing accurately.

What about the goalie?

If you're defending against a free kick, you need to decide on who is in the defensive wall. Make sure your players listen to your instructions and tell them where to stand and whether they have to move as you make your angles.

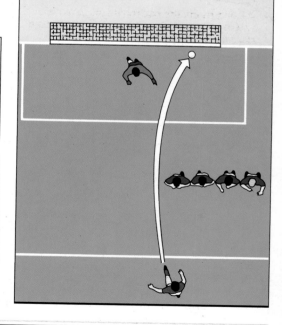

Corner Tactics

Soccer is at its most exciting with goalmouth action, and corners offer the perfect opportunity for a team to create danger here. A corner kick should always lead to a shot at goal. Practise different routines when you're training and always make the most of your team's skills. If you've got a good header — use him!

● If you know your opponents are good in the air, vary your corners.
Attacking the near post or sending a low drive into the crowded area are useful options.

● Remember that you can't be offside directly from a corner kick, so if you're receiving the kick you can shoot even if there are not two defenders between you and the goal.

● Because the area is crowded, it's often best to aim for a specific area rather than an individual.

● Don't put the ball where the goalkeeper can come out and catch it easily.

● Corners that swerve in flight are the hardest to defend against. And those that swerve *away* from the goal are good for attacking players who can time their runs to come in and meet them.

● Corners that put the ball close to the posts are hard to defend against.

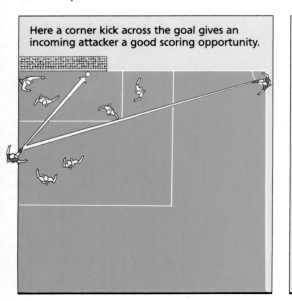

Here a corner kick across the goal gives an incoming attacker a good scoring opportunity.

What about the goalie?

Goalkeepers have a lot of responsibility at corners telling their defenders where to be. You'll probably find it useful to have two defenders on the goal line covering the inside of each post.

Penalty Tactics

It is often said that nobody should miss a penalty. The odds are certainly stacked against the keeper. Yet at all levels players regularly miss penalties, often at the cost of the match. Following a few simple rules should help ensure your success:

If you're kicking a penalty . . .

● Make sure you shut out any distractions and comments around you and just concentrate on kicking the ball accurately.

● Decide where you're going to place the ball and hit it firmly. Don't change your mind as you step up to take the kick.

● Try to disguise your intentions. In the picture opposite the player runs up in line with the left-hand post but kicks the ball in the *opposite* direction.

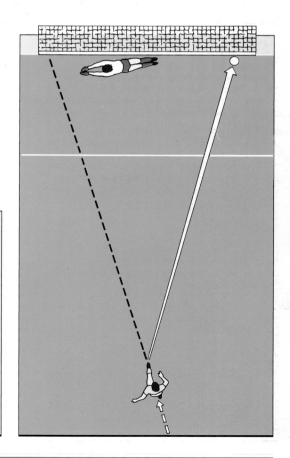

What about the goalie?

In theory you have no chance of stopping a penalty. Yet keepers continually DO stop them — why? The answer is, mainly luck and some very quick reactions! Most keepers will decide which way to dive and hurl themselves in the direction in the hope of getting a touch of some sort. This really is the only way — and it sometimes works!

Fitness

You need to be fit to play soccer — especially when you realise that during the 90 minutes of a match you will be running about five miles (eight kms). As well as being fast on your feet, you need to be able to stop, start and change direction quickly.

Before puberty, players do not need any special fitness training — playing the game and practising ball control skills will be enough. If you are over sixteen, your coach will help you devise a fitness programme tailored to your needs.

Diet

Whatever your age, your fitness levels will benefit from a good, balanced diet. This need not be difficult or boring — just follow some very basic guidelines:

EAT MORE
- fresh vegetables and fruit.
- wholemeal bread and cereals.
- grilled or baked food.
- bars from health food shops.
- semi-skimmed milk.

EAT LESS
- processed tinned vegetables.
- sliced white bread and sugary cereals.
- fatty or fried food.
- sweets, crisps and fizzy drinks.
- full cream milk.

Injuries

With a contact sport like football, it is inevitable that some minor injuries will occur. If you do hurt a muscle, tendon or ligament, give it the RICE treatment:

Rest — stop using the affected part, otherwise permanent damage may result.

Ice — a cold compress of ice cubes in a cloth or plastic bag will help reduce swelling.

Compression — wrap the injured part in a crepe or elastic bandage, firmly but not too tightly. This again will help keep swelling to a minimum.

Elevation — raise the part to help drain excess fluid and reduce swelling.

If there is no improvement after 48 hours, always seek medical advice.

Warm-up

Warming up with gentle stretching exercises is VITAL before a match — and recommended as preparation before even an informal game with friends. If you play football without stretching your leg muscles first, you are likely to suffer injuries as a result. Your warm-up session should be at least ten minutes long and include:

1 Ankle rotations

Make circular movements with your feet, in both directions. Do five for each foot.

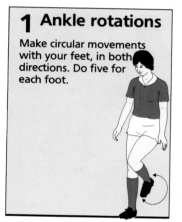

2 Calf and thigh stretches

Kick your legs up behind you, as high as you can. Ten each side. Do the same again, this time holding your foot as shown.

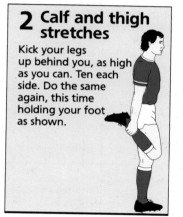

3 Jogging and sprinting

Run around the pitch at a jogging pace, interspersed with short sprints.

4 Groin and hamstring stretches

Stretch one leg out to the side, the other bent as shown and hold for the count of five. Do three each side.

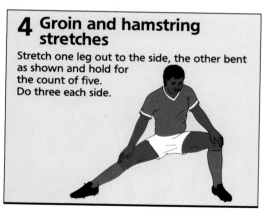

5 Back and stomach stretches

Bending from the foot with your left up and repeat on the side. hip, touch your right hand, then straighten other side. Ten each

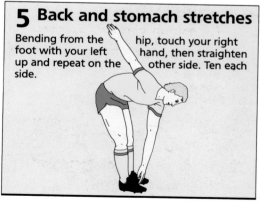

Practice

You should aim to practise all the techniques described on pages 18-37: running with the ball, dribbling, heading and so on. Some you can practise on your own, perhaps against a wall, others will obviously need to be done with friends or team mates.

These pages give you some further ideas for effective and enjoyable practising.

1 Football tennis

For two or more players. You can play this on a real tennis court or improvise with a cord three or four feet (one metre) high and cones or markers to show the court's edges.

● Start with an underhand throw from the baseline.

● Then send the ball back and forth over the net, using any part of your body except your hands.

● The ball can bounce once before you return it.

● For four players, you can allow two or three passes (without a bounce) between players in one side before sending the ball across the net.

2 Head tennis

For two or four players

● Set up as before, but this time only headers are allowed.

● You can adapt the game according to your skill levels — for example, team members could head to each other before returning the serve over the net.

3 Throw-head-catch

For three or six players. The idea is to score goals by heading. The first ball is thrown, the receiver must head it and the next receiver must catch it. The opposition try to intercept. If they do, they must then throw it, head it and catch it.

Juggling

Keeping the ball in the air without touching it with your hands is a great way to improve your 'feel' for the ball, and is good for all-round fitness too. Practise the different variations described in this chart, which you can also use to record your progress. You'll be surprised how quickly you will improve with regular practice!

Skill practice chart

- Write in your best score for each week.
- Each touch on the ball counts as one.

- Once the ball has touched the ground you must start again.
- You can start by playing the ball from your hands or any way you like.

SKILL	Week 1	Week 2	Week 3	Week 4	Week 5	Aim at	Personal best
Ball juggling Any part of body except hands							
Tap-ups Feet only							
Thigh-ups Thigh only							
Head-ups Head only							

Glossary

ANGLES Applied to the direction in which the ball travels. Goalkeepers constantly calculate the angles and get into a position which 'narrows the angles' for the shooter.

BALL WATCHING Watching the ball to the exclusion of your opponent.

BLIND SIDE The side of a player away from the ball or an opponent.

BLOCK TACKLE A tackle made from an upright position with the inside of the foot.

BOX The penalty area.

BY-LINE The goal line.

CHIP A kick with a high trajectory and backspin useful for passing over a defensive *wall*.

CLOSE DOWN To hem in an opponent.

CROSS Kicking the ball towards the penalty area from a wide position.

CROSS OVER Two players on the attacking side passing each other in different directions.

CUSHION To control the ball by relaxing the part of the body in contact with it, in the direction the ball is travelling.

'D' The arc at the edge of the penalty area.

DEAD BALL One that is kicked from a stationary position.

DEFENSIVE WALL The wall of players who line up in defence to prevent the attacking side from gaining an advantage on a free kick. The wall must line up at least 10yds from where the kick is taken.

DUMMY A fake move in one direction when dribbling or passing, when actually going the opposite way to confuse the defender (*Feint*).

FAR POST The goal post furthest from the player with the ball.

FEINT A deceptive movement.

FLANK The area of pitch near the touchlines.

FIFA International Federation of Football Associations.

KILLING THE BALL Making the ball stop, by *TRAPPING* or other means.

LOFTED DRIVE A high pass made by kicking the bottom half of the ball with your instep.

MAN-FOR-MAN *Marking* one particular opponent.

MARKING Keeping close to an opposing player, making it hard for him to get away or to receive a pass.

MARKING-UP To take up *marking* positions.

NEAR POST The goal post nearer to the player with the ball.

ONE TOUCH Passing the ball on straight away without getting it under control first.

ONE-TWO Quick passes between two players.

OVERLAP To go past a team mate who has the ball, ready to take up an attacking position.

SCREEN To shield the ball from an opponent to stop him gaining possession.

SET PIECE Well-practised routines from DEAD BALL situations.

STRIKER An attacking player whose main job is to score goals.

SWEEPER A defender operating at the back of the defence.

TRAP To control the ball.

THROUGH BALL A pass through the defence to an attacking player running towards the goal.

TWO TOUCH Getting the ball under control before passing it (cf *one touch*).

VOLLEY A kick which makes contact with the ball while it is still in the air.

WALL see *Defensive wall*

WALL PASS A pass which uses a team mate to 'bounce' a pass back to you.